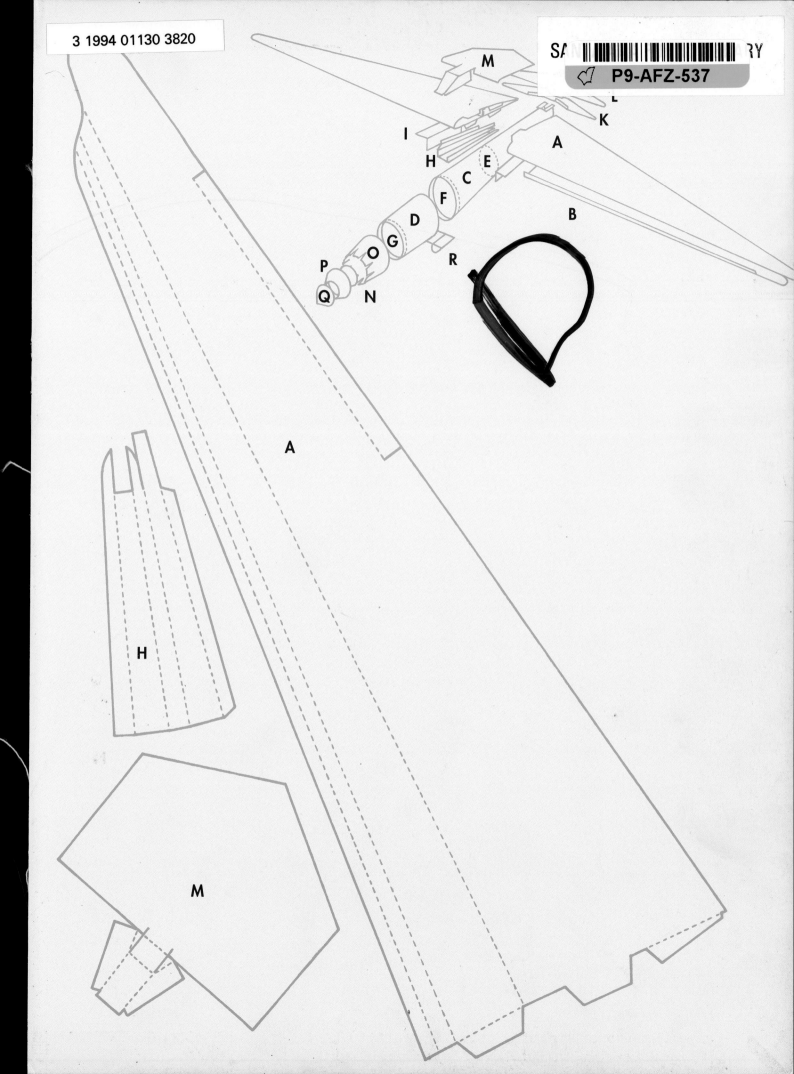

HOW SCIENCE WORKS

PLANES

AND OTHER AIRCRAFT

NIGEL HAWKES

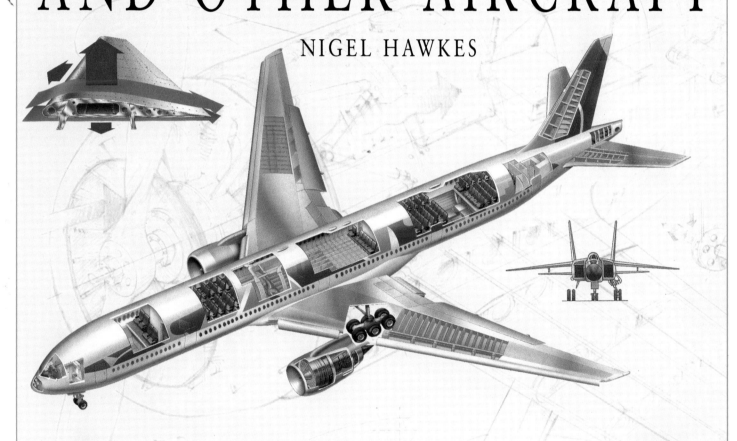

COPPER BEECH BOOKS

BROOKFIELD • CONNECTICUT

CONTENTS

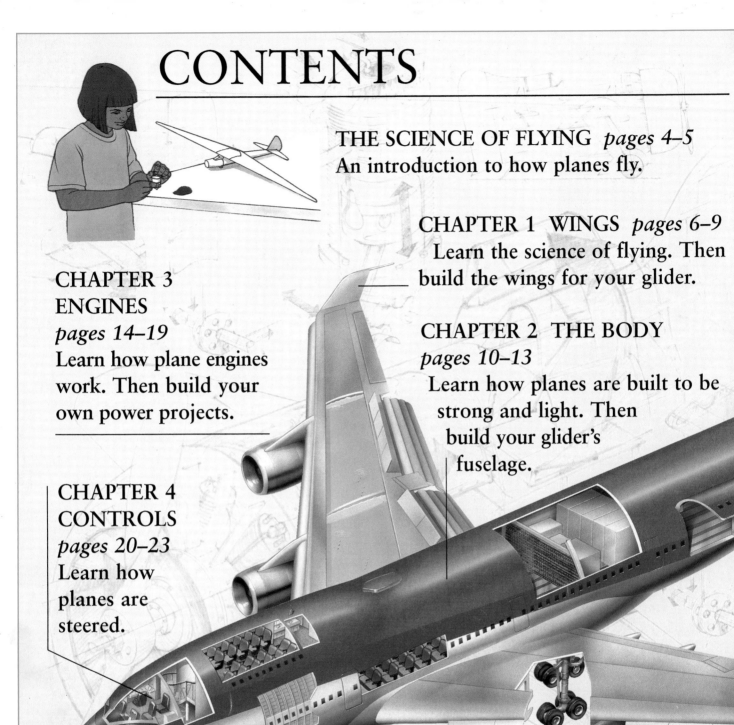

Boeing 747 Jumbo

INTRODUCTION

Airplanes come in all shapes and sizes. Yet the smallest one–person craft and biggest jumbo jet fly in much the same way. Most planes use the flow of air over their wings to provide lift, and propellers or jets to drive them forward. Look inside planes and helicopters, and see for yourself the science behind how they work. Each chapter comes with a project. If you do them all, you can build a fantastic glider that really flies!

To make the glider you will need: paper, thin cardboard, scissors, tape, craft glue, pencil, ruler, and modeling clay. For other projects you will need: thick cardboard, rubber bands, matchsticks, hairdryer, straws, bendy wire, two jar lids, a stick, ballpoint pen, and a candle.

Model glider project box

Science experiment project box

© Aladdin Books
Ltd 1999

Designed and produced by
Aladdin Books Ltd
28 Percy Street
London W1P 0LD

First published in the United States in 1999 by
Copper Beech Books,
an imprint of The Millbrook Press
2 Old New Milford Road
Brookfield, Connecticut 06804

Editor
Jim Pipe

Consultant
Steve Allman

Design
David West
Children's Book Design

Designer
Flick Killerby
Illustrators
Ian Thompson, Ross Watton, Rob Shone, Alex Pang

Picture Research
Brooks Krikler Research

Printed in Belgium

Library of Congress Cataloging-in-Publication Data
Hawkes, Nigel, 1943–
Planes and other aircraft/Nigel Hawkes.
p. cm. – – (How science works)
Includes index.
Summary: Explains the basic science of flight, the problems of getting vehicles into the air, different types of engine, and aircraft design. Includes instructions for making aircraft models.
ISBN 0–7613–3260–X (lib. bdg.)
– – 0–7613–0826–1 (pbk.)
1. Airplanes Juvenile literature.
2. Helicopters Juvenile literature.
[1. Airplanes. 2. Flight] I. Title. II Series.
TL547.H38 1999   99–37560
629.133'34– –dc21   CIP

THE SCIENCE OF FLYING

A modern jet has a lot of controls to ensure safety.

Two things must happen if a plane is going to fly. First, the lift from its wings must be greater than its weight. Second, it needs to travel fast enough for its wings to work. To do this, the thrust of its engines must be bigger than the drag of the air that holds it back.

LIFT

Air flowing over the wings lifts a plane upward. Wings work mainly because of their airfoil shape – a rounded top surface and a flatter bottom surface. Turn to page 7 to make a wing shape.

DRAG

DRAG

When you cycle fast, you can feel the force of the air pushing against you and slowing you down. This is known as drag. How much drag a plane creates depends on its shape and smoothness.

Wings create drag as well as lift, and the faster the plane goes, the more drag it creates.

Wright Flyer I

Most planes have a tail plane at the back. But the Wright Brothers' Flyer 1, the first powered plane, had a tail plane in front.

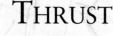
Tristar airliner

ALL CHANGE

The forces on a plane change all the time. For example, fuel makes a big difference to a plane's weight. As it gets used up, the plane becomes lighter. Voyager, the first plane to fly around the world non-stop, weighed almost four times as much when its fuel tanks were full up.

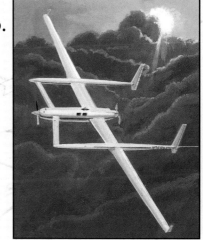
Voyager

THRUST

Both propellers and jets work by driving a large amount of air backward, which has the effect of pushing the plane forward. Turn to page 14 to find out how jets work.

LIFT

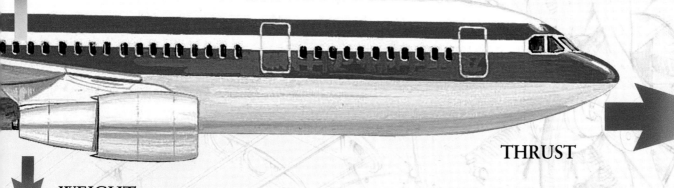

THRUST

WEIGHT

WEIGHT

The weight of the plane, its passengers (*left*), luggage, and fuel all pull the plane downward.

The best planes are made from very light materials that are also very strong. To see how planes are put together, turn to page 10.

Helicopter rotors provide lift, like wings. When tilted slightly, they push the helicopter forward. Read all about helicopters on page 17.

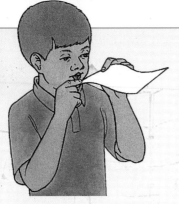

CHAPTER 1 – WINGS

Wings create lift in two ways: by their airfoil shape, and by the angle at which they are set. Air rushing past the wing creates the lift. But the flow of air must be smooth.

Increasing the angle of the wing increases lift, but only up to a point. Too great an angle causes turbulence, making the wing "stall" and lose lift (page 25).

A piece of paper can work like a wing. Hold it in front of your mouth and blow across the top surface. This lifts the paper upward, because the air on top is moving faster.

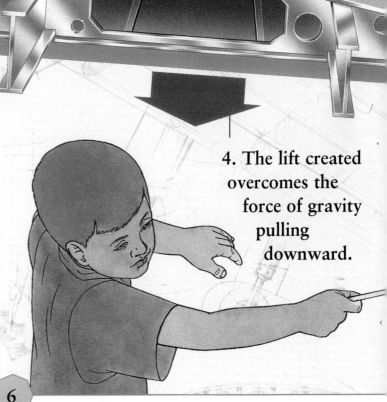

3. Low pressure caused by the faster flow above the wing creates lift.

1. Wings move through the air.

4. The lift created overcomes the force of gravity pulling downward.

AIRFOILS

Most wings are airfoils. This means that they have a rounded upper surface and a flatter bottom surface. This special shape works like this:

1. As the plane moves forward, the air flows both under and over it.
2. Air flowing over the wing moves faster than that below it.
3. This creates an area of low pressure above the wing, sucking it upward.

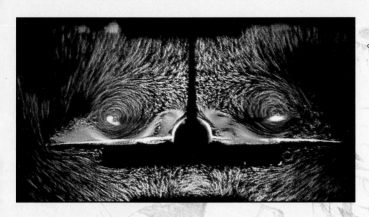

WIND TEST

Wind tunnels are used to test how air flows over a wing. The Concorde's unusual wings produce vortices – little whirlpools of air near the tips for extra lift at low speeds.

2. The shape of the wing forces air flowing over it to go faster than the air flowing below.

FEEL THE FORCE

Test your model wing by pulling it through the air. You will feel it rising in your hand as the air rushes over it. Then alter the angle of the wing. Does this affect the amount of lift it produces?

MODEL PLANE
PART 1
WINGS

1 It's time to put the science into action. At the ends of the book are plans to build your glider. Just photocopy or transfer them onto paper and cut the shapes out. Ask an adult to help as careful cutting will make your plane fly better. To start, cut out wing shape **A**, and score along the dotted lines.

2 Carefully fold the edge of piece **A** into an L-shape (*above*). Glue this L-shape down, and pull it slightly toward the opposite edge. This makes the curved airfoil shape that gives your glider lift (*right*).

3 Cut out wing part **B** and fold it along the dotted line. Then glue it to **A**, next to the part that has been folded over (*above*). Make sure the ends of **A** and **B** line up correctly.

4 To make the other wing, cut out parts **A** and **B** and turn them over. Fold along the dotted lines in the opposite direction, and glue as you did on the first wing. Check that you have made both left and right wings.

WING SHAPES

Flaps

Slots

Fokker triplane

You know that the basic wing shape is rounded on top and flat underneath. But wings vary a lot, depending on the plane. Fast fighters get all the lift they need from small wings. Jumbo jets need large wings with flaps and slots to give extra lift at low speed.

CREATING MORE LIFT

Designers have tried all sorts of wing shapes. The Concorde has triangular delta wings for supersonic flight. Short takeoff and landing (STOL) planes have broad wings for extra lift.

Modern gliders (*left*) use advanced materials to make their long, thin wings strong enough.

Glider

MOVING WINGS

For high speed, a swept-back wing is best for reducing drag. But it creates less lift at takeoff and landing. Some fighters have "swing wings." These are hinged so that they can fly well, both quickly and slowly. But the system costs too much to use in airliners.

Tornados

Swing wing in backward position

Swing wing in forward position

TIGHT TURNS

Many early planes had two or more wings, one above the other (*left*). These created more lift than a single wing and allowed the pilot to make tight turns. These planes are still used today for stunt flying.

Martin X-24B

Some modern planes have swept-forward wings that also allow very tight turns at high speed.

The stealth plane's shape is hard for radar to pick up (see page 27).

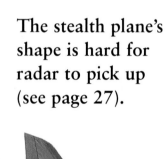

Some aircraft have a "flying wing" shape (*above*). The shape of the whole airplane acts like an airfoil.

HELICOPTERS

Helicopter rotors are like thin wings whirling through the air. By tilting them slightly, the helicopter can move in any direction.

Lift

Direction of spin

N31976

Helicopters are slower than fast jets. But they can hover and go places normal planes can't.

Spinning whirligig

1 To make a wing, cut out a piece of paper 4 in x 2 $\frac{1}{2}$ in. Fold it over a straw so that one side is curved like an airfoil. Then make another wing and attach this to the other end of the straw.
2 With tape, attach the straw to another straw at a right angle. Attach a lump of modeling clay to the bottom of the second straw. Hold the whirligig with the blades at the top. If you brush your hands together quickly, the blades spin and the whirligig flies up.

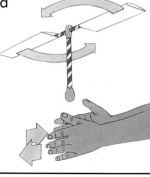

CHAPTER 2 – THE BODY

Early planes were made of wood, held together by wire, and covered in a fabric skin that added nothing to their strength (*right*). They often had two short wings, because these materials couldn't make a long wing strong enough.

A big change came when the skin of the plane became part of the structure, and metal was used instead of wood. This skin fitted over a framework of ribs and frames.

Strength

1 A sheet of thin cardboard seems to have little strength. If you roll it into a tube around two jar lids, it is still easily bent (*below*). But glue rings of thick cardboard to it, and it has strength in one direction.

2 Glue strips of cardboard to the tube for strength in the other direction (*below*). It is now much more difficult to bend or crush, even though it is made of cardboard. This is how a plane's fuselage is built. But since it is made from metal it is incredibly strong.

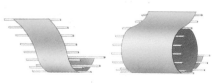

Rib

Frame | Skin

B-17 Flying Fortress

METAL SKIN

The B-17 Flying Fortress (*main picture*) used aluminum alloys for ribs, frames, and skin in the 1940s. Today, most planes are made in a similar way.

Sikorsky
Le Grand

UNDER PRESSURE

Have you been on a fairground ride and felt the pressure on your body as you spin around? These centrifugal forces act on a plane every time it turns in the air. This is why a plane needs to be strong as well as light.

The ribs in the fuselage (body) and the struts in the wings have circles cut out of them to make them lighter.

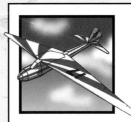

MODEL PLANE
PART 2

FUSELAGE

1 Two sections make up the fuselage of your glider – parts **C** and **D**. Like a real plane, they are strengthened by frames – **E**, **F**, and **G**. To make **C**, roll it into a tube, then glue it.

2 Make part **D** the same way. Then cut out **E**, **F**, and **G** from cardboard. Push frame **E** down into **C** using a straw, until it is wedged in. Then glue **F** and **G** just inside the openings of **C** and **D**. This should leave an overlap so that **C** slips over **D**. Glue parts **C** and **D** together.

tail flaps

3 After this, fold **H** along the dotted lines as shown (*below*). Then glue **H** over the join of **C** and **D**. But make sure **H** lines up with the tail flaps on the top of **C**.

4 You have now made the main body and the wings. Turn to page 20 to join them together.

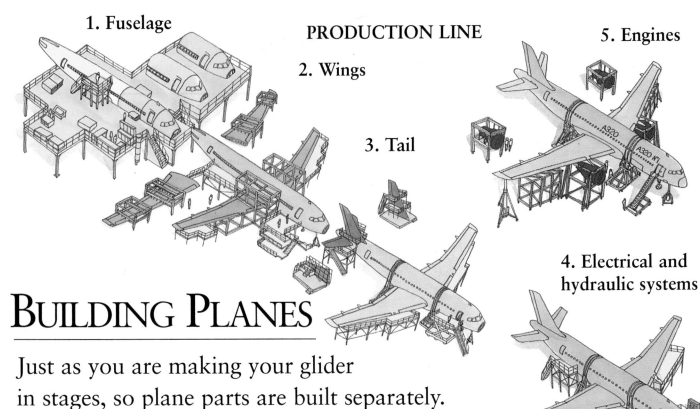

1. Fuselage

PRODUCTION LINE

2. Wings

3. Tail

5. Engines

4. Electrical and hydraulic systems

BUILDING PLANES

Just as you are making your glider in stages, so plane parts are built separately. They are often made in different factories, then brought together for assembly. The fuselage forms the main structure. Then wings, tail, and engines are attached. Smooth, simple shapes are the easiest to make, and also the strongest.

LIGHT AND STRONG

Modern airliners are made mainly of aluminum alloys (mixtures of metals). Titanium is tougher, but more expensive. It is used around jet engines and for wing leading edges. Plastics form floors and seats. New materials such as Kevlar and carbon fiber are very light, and stronger than steel.

FIGHTER MIX
- Carbon Fiber
- Kevlar
- Titanium
- Aluminum/lithium
- Steel

Carbon fiber is made of millions of fibers. They are set in a tough resin (glue). Each layer has its fibers laid in a different direction.

PRODUCTION LINE

An airliner is built in stages (*left*):
1 The fuselage is made in sections and put together with rivets or glue.
2 The wings are attached to the body.
3 The tail section is added.
4 Then the fuel pipes and electrical and hydraulic systems are linked up.
5 The plane's engines are added.

A wing is tested to see when it breaks.

Every part has to resist fatigue – even the windows.

The Comet 1 (*above*) had square windows. Pressure at the corners started cracks that caused two crashes.

TESTING THE PARTS

Parts are regularly tested. Most tests try to make sure that a part will not fail due to fatigue – the constant bending back and forth as the plane flies. Fatigue creates cracks, which grow until the part breaks. Try bending a paper clip again and again: how long does it last?

SUPER GLUE

Rivets are strong, but cause local stresses that can turn into cracks. Welding (melting metal to stick parts together) is tricky to do and difficult to check. Many planes today are in fact stuck together with very strong glues.

CHAPTER 3 – ENGINES

Wings need air rushing past them to create lift. So planes need to be driven forward by pushing lots of air back. Both propellers and jet engines use angled spinning blades that cut through the air and push it backward. Propeller planes use less fuel but fly more slowly. Jets are more powerful, with greater speed and range.

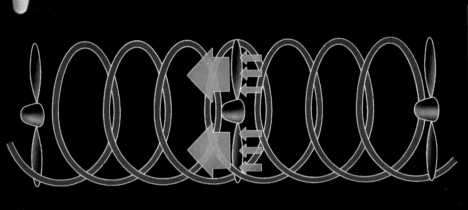

As the propeller spins, the air pressure in front of it drops. The high pressure behind pushes the plane forward. The blades are curved to act like screws being driven through the air.

PROPELLERS

Propeller blades are shaped like wings, with an airfoil section. They are made from aluminum, carbon fiber, and plastic.

Two, three, or four blades make up each propeller. On most planes, the angle (or pitch) of each blade can be changed to produce the best performance for climbing or cruising.

High pitch creates little drag and is used for cruising.

Low pitch creates thrust at takeoff.

The Dornier Do X, the biggest plane of its time, had twelve piston engines – six pulling, six pushing. Even so, they only just gave it enough power to take off.

Pushing air

Cut a propeller shape out of cardboard, twisting it at both ends to make an airfoil shape. Then wrap a piece of bendy wire around the middle. Attach this to a rubber band, and pull it through an empty pen case. Then slip a matchstick over the end. Holding the match with one hand, twist the propeller around and around. Then let go and feel it blow your face (*left*).

JET ENGINES

Jet engines suck in air at one end and force it out of the other at very high speed. They work by mixing fuel with air and burning it. As it burns, the mix expands and pours out of the back of the engine. The gases that rush backward thrust the plane in the opposite direction – forward.

A TURBOJET ENGINE

1. Air is sucked into the front of the engine by a spinning fan called a compressor.

2. The space narrows as the air flows into the engine, squeezing it and making it hotter.

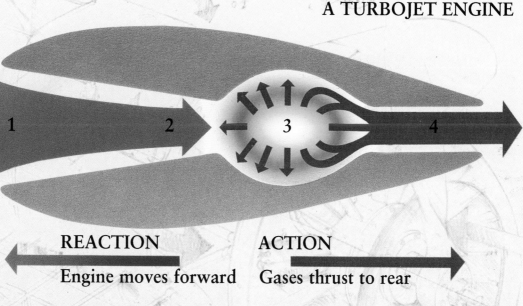

REACTION
Engine moves forward

ACTION
Gases thrust to rear

3. As air enters the combustion chamber, nozzles spray in fuel, which is ignited (set alight).

4. The burning mixture expands, and hot gases roar out the back, creating thrust.

The big squeeze

1. Modern jet engines use the simple principle of compressing (squeezing) air. The air is taken in through a large opening. This narrows, making the air speed up.
2. Try this using a hairdryer set to cold – but ask an adult to help. Can it blow out a candle 5 feet away? The air spreads out so it probably can't.
3. But if you put a cardboard funnel shape over the dryer, the faster stream should blow out the candle.

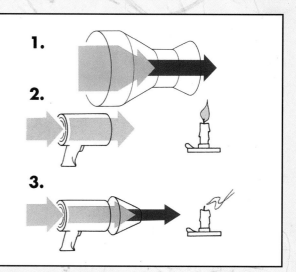

1.

2.

3.

THE PISTON ENGINE

A piston engine works by sucking fuel and air into the cylinder. It then sets it alight with an electric spark. The explosion forces the piston down. The piston is connected to a shaft that drives the propeller. Several cylinders often work together, firing one after the other to spin the propeller around.

In a six-cylinder engine (*above*), the pistons are laid flat. But in older planes they were often arranged in a circle (*below*).

Piston engines are widely used on smaller aircraft that need to save fuel rather than fly fast (*left*).

PROPELLER PLANES

Propellers are used by light planes or short-distance passenger planes. They are usually driven by four-stroke piston engines, more powerful versions of those that power a car. Helicopters use propellers in the form of rotors. These are driven by piston engines or turbojets.

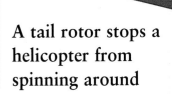

A tail rotor stops a helicopter from spinning around

ROTORS AND PROPELLERS

The V-22 Osprey tries to combine the advantages of an airplane and a helicopter. It has engines that rotate so that it can take off vertically, using its propellers like a helicopter's rotors. Then it swings its engines 90 degrees to turn into an airplane.

TWISTING ROTORS

Rotor blades are controlled by a swashplate. **Swashplate**
Tilting the swashplate changes the angle of
the rotors. This makes the helicopter go up
or down, forward or back (*right*).

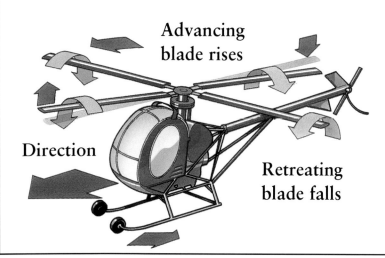

Advancing
blade rises

Direction

Retreating
blade falls

As each rotor blade travels toward
the front of the helicopter, the air
flowing over it increases (*left*). This
creates lift, and the blade tip rises.
As it travels to the back, the tip
falls. This makes the blades flap up
and down as they spin around.

Gearbox

Turbojet

Main rotor

HELICOPTER ENGINES

Modern helicopters
use turbojets to
drive the main rotor and the
tail rotor. The turbojet
engines suck air in. They
squeeze it, mix it with
fuel, then set it alight. The
hot gases spin a turbine
(fan), which is linked to
both rotors by a gearbox.

Shaft
connects
engine to
tail rotor

AUTOGYRO

The autogyro uses a free-spinning rotor
as a wing. As the autogyro propeller
drives it forward, the rotor spins to
create lift. However, the autogyro
cannot hover like a helicopter.

Autogyro

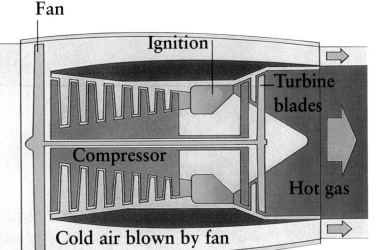

Fan

Ignition

Turbine blades

Compressor

Hot gas

Cold air blown by fan

A turbofan works by sucking cold air in, compressing it, and mixing it with fuel. After being ignited, the hot gases shoot out of the engine and spin the turbine blades.

The turbine is joined to a shaft that drives the front fan and the compressor. The fan thrusts a mass of cold air around the side of the engine.

JET ENGINES

There is less difference between propeller planes and jets than there seems. Many modern jets are turbofans. In these engines, most of the thrust comes from cold air blown around the engine by a large fan at the front. Turbofans are quieter and cost less to run than turbojets.

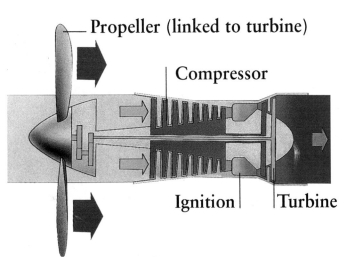

Propeller (linked to turbine)

Compressor

Ignition

Turbine

Turboprops (*above*) are more expensive than piston engines, but are smaller, lighter, and use less fuel.

TURBOPROPS

Small airliners (*below*) use turboprops. They have propellers linked to turbojets, with thrust coming both from the propeller and the jet.

Jets set for level flight

Jets set for takeoff and landing

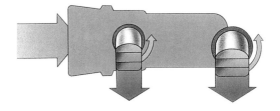

THRUST REVERSAL

To stop quickly once they have landed, airliners use scoops, which direct the thrust from their engines forward. This means they can land on much shorter runways.

JUMP JETS

The Harrier jump jet (*below*) can swivel its jet thrust, allowing it to take off and land vertically, as well as avoid attack by making sudden changes of direction while flying.

X-15 rocket plane

ROCKET POWER

At high altitudes the air runs out, so jets will not work. Rockets carry all their fuel with them, burning it to produce thrust even in deep space. But carrying so much fuel makes rockets incredibly expensive and leaves little room for cargo.

CHAPTER 4 – CONTROLS

To fly planes safely, pilots must be able to control the air flowing over the wings and the tail. To do so, they use hinged flaps — ailerons on the trailing edge of wings, elevators on the tail, and a rudder on the fin. These redirect the flow of air to create forces that make the plane go where the pilot wants. For example, the plane is turned by rolling it with the ailerons at the same time as turning the rudder.

Adjusting your glider's ailerons

MODEL PLANE
PART 3
ADDING THE WINGS

1 Add the wings to the body. Glue the tabs on the end of each wing to the top of the fuselage above section **H**.

2 Glue part **I** under both wings.

Slots

Spoilers

Aileron

Flaps

YAW
The rudder controls the direction the plane is pointing, called yaw. It helps the plane stay on course in windy conditions.

ROLL
Ailerons roll the plane from side to side. Some aerobatic planes can complete a roll, all the way around, in a single second.

PITCH
Pitch is the angle the plane points above or below the horizon. The pilot controls it using the elevators on the tail.

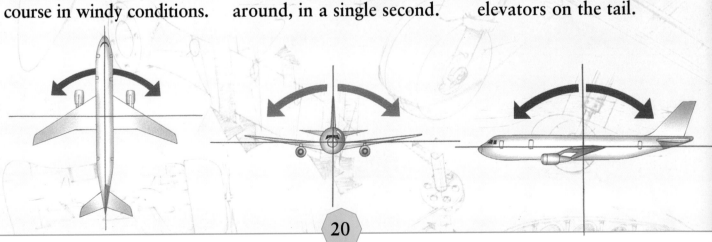

FLYING YOUR GLIDER

The basic control surfaces are the same with your glider. The rudder and tail are so sensitive you can just bend them to control pitch and yaw. To control roll, cut ailerons into the wings and fold along the dotted lines. See how your glider changes direction when you move the control surfaces.

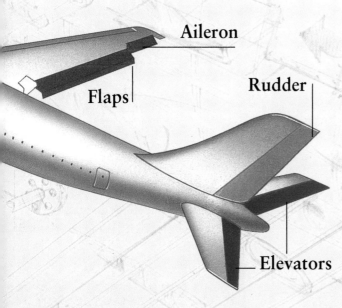

Aileron

Flaps

Rudder

Elevators

EXTRA CONTROLS

Airliners also have big flaps to extend the wing and increase lift. Slots are the movable leading edges on the wing. They increase lift at slow speeds.

Spoilers are flaps that appear just after touchdown. They reduce lift so the tires carry the weight of the plane, and the brakes work effectively.

MODEL PLANE
PART 4
TAIL PLANE

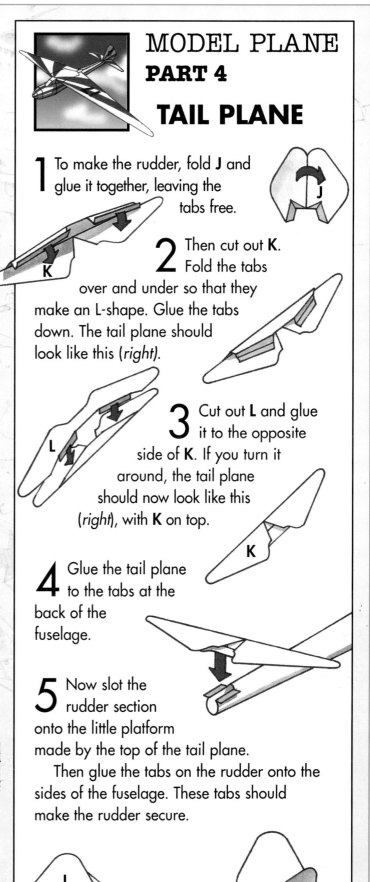

1 To make the rudder, fold **J** and glue it together, leaving the tabs free.

2 Then cut out **K**. Fold the tabs over and under so that they make an L-shape. Glue the tabs down. The tail plane should look like this (*right*).

3 Cut out **L** and glue it to the opposite side of **K**. If you turn it around, the tail plane should now look like this (*right*), with **K** on top.

4 Glue the tail plane to the tabs at the back of the fuselage.

5 Now slot the rudder section onto the little platform made by the top of the tail plane.

Then glue the tabs on the rudder onto the sides of the fuselage. These tabs should make the rudder secure.

21

CONTROL SYSTEMS

In the most modern airliners, the pilot movements are sent to the flaps and elevators electronically (*right*).

This "fly-by-wire" arrangement makes cockpit design easier and takes up less space. In the cockpit itself, the old mechanical dials are being replaced by computer screens.

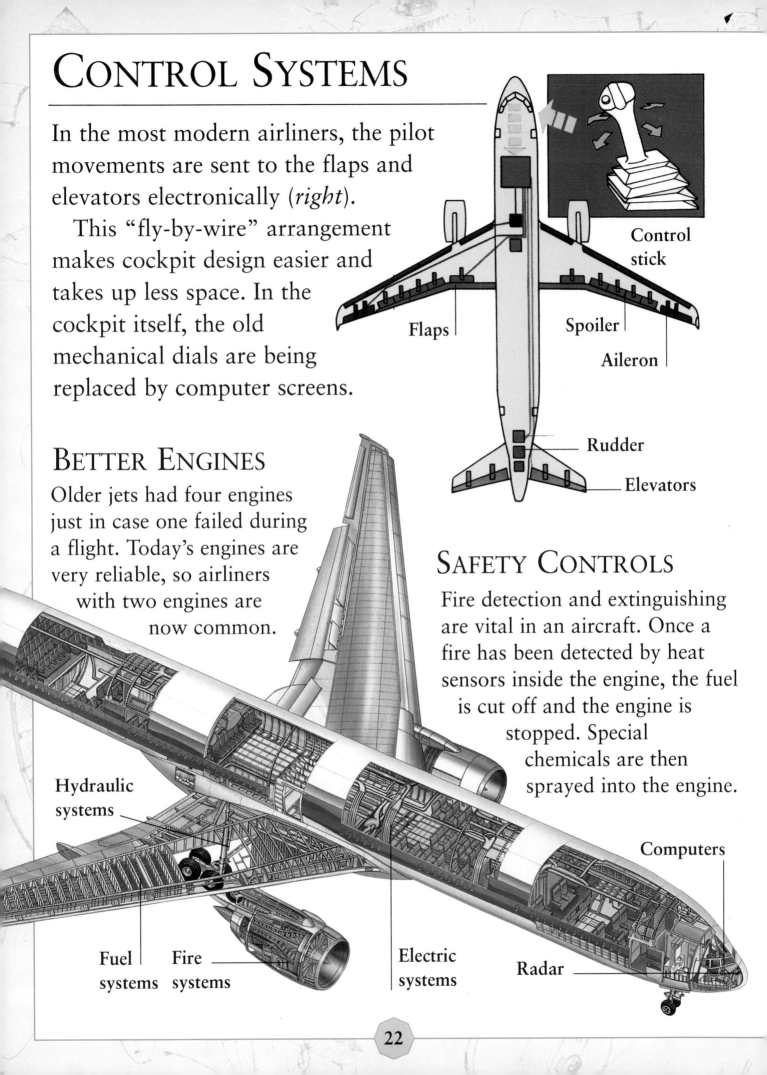

Control stick

Flaps

Spoiler

Aileron

Rudder

Elevators

BETTER ENGINES

Older jets had four engines just in case one failed during a flight. Today's engines are very reliable, so airliners with two engines are now common.

SAFETY CONTROLS

Fire detection and extinguishing are vital in an aircraft. Once a fire has been detected by heat sensors inside the engine, the fuel is cut off and the engine is stopped. Special chemicals are then sprayed into the engine.

Hydraulic systems

Computers

Fuel systems

Fire systems

Electric systems

Radar

AIRBUS COCKPIT
Here are the main cockpit controls:

1 Ignition
2 Radar
3 EADI (page 26)
4 Control stick
5 Thrust levers

However, the autopilot is used for most of the flight, although one pilot is always keeping an eye on the control panels.

NERVE CENTER

At the front of most planes is the cockpit, or flight deck. The first pilot (captain) and second pilot sit in the two front seats. They share the basic flying and navigating roles. Electronic equipment monitors the engines. A special computer, the autopilot, can fly the plane on its own.

TAIL FLYING

YF-22

The YF-22 is an advanced fighter aircraft with a very sophisticated fly-by-wire control system. This allows the pilot to attempt things that are impossible on other planes, such as flying the plane "on its tail."

Early flyers such as the Wright brothers controlled their planes by twisting the wings with wires (*right*). This method may be used in future planes in place of ailerons, flaps, and elevators, using electronic fly-by-wire controls (*above*).

You may need to add some modeling clay to the nose of your plane to balance it.

A jumbo jet's controls are most important during takeoff and landing. Today's airports are very busy, so the pilot needs to be able to take off and land safely in a very short space of time. As the plane taxies out to the runway, you can always see the pilot giving the ailerons, elevators, and rudder a final check.

MAXIMUM LIFT

The engines are always operated at full power on takeoff, though this can be very noisy. The wing flaps are fully extended to increase the size of the wing. This gives the maximum possible lift at a time when the aircraft is heaviest, with a full load of fuel.

Flow of air while the plane speeds up

Flow of air at takeoff

GAINING SPEED
When the wings are angled slightly, they don't create much lift. But they don't produce much drag either. This helps the airliner to speed up on takeoff.

TAKEOFF
When the plane is traveling fast enough to take off, the nose of the aircraft is pulled up. This sudden change in the angle of the wings creates a lot of lift.

MODEL PLANE
PART 5

COCKPIT & NOSE

Here are the final two sections for building the plane – adding the cockpit section and the nose. If you want to paint your plane, use paints that aren't water-based (the water will crinkle the paper).

2 To make the nose section, glue the two ends of **O** together, then the two ends of **P**. Slot **P** over **O** and glue inside using the tabs. Glue **Q** to **P**. **BUT** don't glue the nose on until you have tested for balance (page 24).

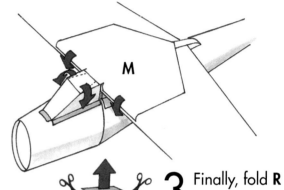

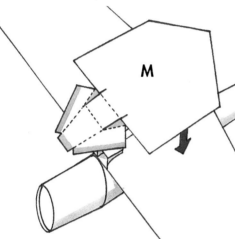

1 Cut out section **M**, the cockpit. Bend the sides under the top and glue it down onto the top of the wings. This section also strengthens the join between the wings and the body.

3 Finally, fold **R** into an accordion shape and glue the folds together. Cut the edges off with scissors to make a round shape, and glue **R** to the body where **C** meets **D**. Turn to page 21 for flying tips.

STALLING

However, if the nose is pulled up too much, a stall can occur. Air stops flowing across the upper surface so the wings stop producing lift. Air flowing under the wing creates more drag. A plane can drop out of the sky if it stalls.

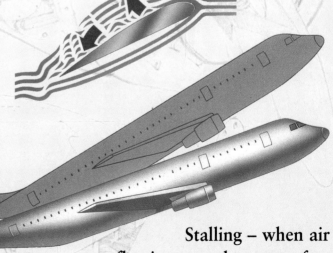

Stalling – when air flowing over the top surface of the wing breaks away

LANDING AT SEA

To land on water, some aircraft have floats instead of wheels, or bodies shaped like boats. To land on an aircraft carrier, fighters have a special hook that is caught by ropes stretched across the deck.

A Chinook helicopter drops its load before landing.

THE LANDING

When landing, the autopilot picks up two sets of beams, which guide the plane in. At about 60 feet from the ground, the pilot brings the plane's nose up to slow it down. Once the plane touches down, the pilot uses brakes, spoilers, and reverse thrust to bring it to a halt.

Even on automatic pilot, the crew watch their instruments carefully. An altimeter shows height, the ASI (air speed indicator) shows speed, a compass shows direction, and the EADI (electronic attitude director indicator) shows if the plane is level.

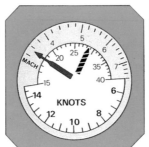
ASI

Compass

EADI

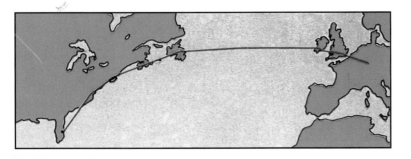

Long flight paths take into account the round shape of the earth and air currents such as the jet stream. These high-altitude winds can make a journey much faster in one direction.

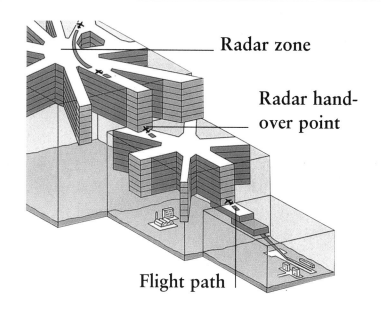

Radar zone

Radar hand-over point

Flight path

STACKING PLANES

If an airliner cannot come straight in for a landing, it is diverted into a stack a few miles from the airport. Here, waiting aircraft circle at different levels, slowly flying down as earlier aircraft are called to break off and approach the runway. In busy airports, a plane will take off or land every minute.

RADAR

Airliners are brought in to land using radar beams to keep them on the right flight path. Air traffic controllers (*right*) bring in the planes one at a time, keeping a safe distance between them. The planes appear on the radar screen as glowing green dots (*above*).

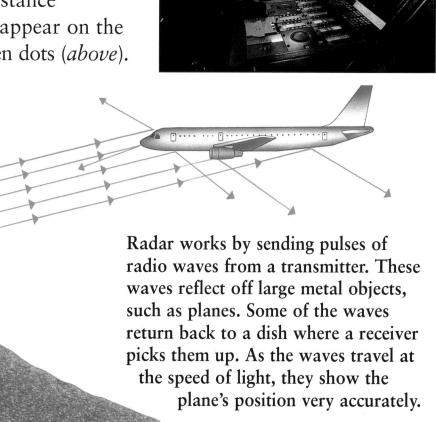

A radar transmitter and receiver spins constantly.

Radar works by sending pulses of radio waves from a transmitter. These waves reflect off large metal objects, such as planes. Some of the waves return back to a dish where a receiver picks them up. As the waves travel at the speed of light, they show the plane's position very accurately.

GRAVITY

Gravity is a natural force that pulls objects toward each other. It is tiny – two 1-pound weights a foot apart attract each other with a force of only 1 billionth of an ounce. But the earth is so huge that it creates a big pull down toward its center. We feel this force as weight.

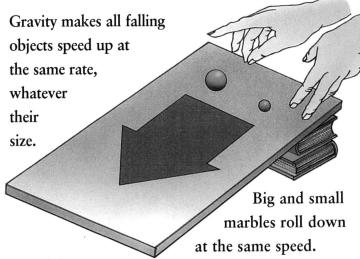

Gravity makes all falling objects speed up at the same rate, whatever their size.

Big and small marbles roll down at the same speed.

> **?** *1 Which plane do you think will fall faster because of gravity — a jumbo or a glider?*

LIFT

Planes overcome the force of gravity by creating lift. Air flowing over their wings creates an upward force greater than the force of gravity, so the plane lifts off the ground. The larger and heavier the plane, the greater the lift must be.

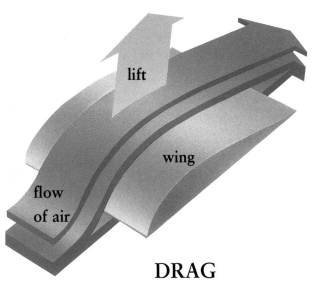

lift

wing

flow of air

> **?** *2 Why are wings curved along the top, and nearly flat along the bottom? Answers to all the questions on pages 28–29 are on page 32.*

DRAG

Air, like water, is a fluid. As an object moves through a fluid, it has to push the fluid out of the way. The fluid resists being pushed, creating a force called drag. The denser the fluid and the faster the object moves, the greater the drag is.

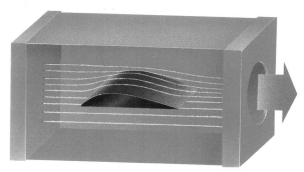

Drag can be tested in a wind tunnel.

THRUST

Nothing moves of its own accord. A plane needs thrust to drive it forward. This must be strong enough to overcome drag. Propellers or jet engines create thrust by driving air backward, pushing the plane forward.

? *3 What sort of engine normally produces the most thrust? Is it a propeller engine, a jet, or a rocket? Turn to page 19 if you need to read about this again.*

RIGID STRUCTURES

Planes must be strong, to resist buffeting and so they can be pressurized inside to make up for the thin air at high altitude. They use a framework of ribs and a strong skin to achieve this. The strength of a material depends partly upon how it is shaped.

A flat piece of cardboard will bend easily under a small force. But curved into a cylinder, or bent into an M-shape (*right*), it is much stronger. This is because the force has to compress the cardboard, not simply bend it.

? *Which shape is the strongest – a square, a circle, or a triangle? To find out, try making them from cardboard.*

TECHNICAL TERMS

Airfoil – the shape a wing needs to be to make air flowing over it create lift.
Altitude – height above the ground.
Compressor – the fan at the front of a jet engine that sucks air into it.
Fluid – any substance that flows easily, including all gases and liquids.
Glider – a plane without an engine.

Glider

Monoplane/Biplane/Triplane – the sets of wings on a plane, arranged one above the other. A monoplane has one, a biplane two, and a triplane — very rare today — three.
Pitch – the angle of a propeller or rotor.
Supersonic – traveling faster than the speed of sound (about 660 mph at 36,000 feet).
Streamlined – smoothly shaped to reduce drag by allowing air to flow easily over it.
Transmitter – a device that sends out signals.
Turbine – a series of blades attached to a shaft. These are turned by the pressure of water or, in the case of jet engines, hot gases.
Turbulence – random air currents that disturb the air flowing over the wing.

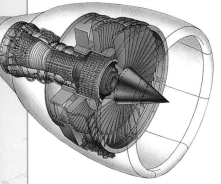

PLANE PARTS

Despite their different purposes, planes have common design features. Experience has shown which of the huge variety of shapes produced by plane designers flies most cheaply, safely, and comfortably.

1. COCKPIT
The pilot and copilot sit side by side in the cockpit of this 20-seat Jetstream. Large planes may also have a third crew member.

2. NOSE
The nose cone is made of plastic so radar signals can pass through it.

3. WING
Monoplanes, with the wings mounted low on the fuselage, are now the most common type.

4. FUSELAGE
The cigar-shaped fuselage gets its strength from its shape and how it is built.

5. ENGINE
Engines are mounted as near the fuselage as possible, to avoid too much turning force if the plane has to fly on one engine in an emergency.

6. PROPELLER
This four-bladed propeller can change its pitch.

7 UNDERCARRIAGE
This monoplane can stow its wheels in the wings during flight. But some other planes have fixed wheels.

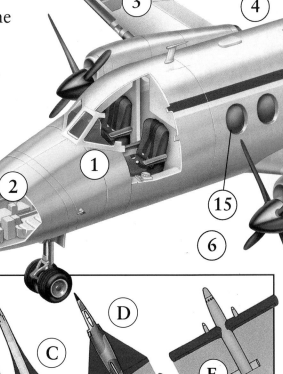

WING SHAPES
A-F show some different wing shapes. Can you find out which are used on the Tornado, Boeing 747 and Martin X-24B? Use the index to track them down. The answers are on page 32.

8. CABIN

The cabin is pressurized so passengers can breathe easily even when the air outside is thin.

9. STAIRS

Stairs mounted in a door can quickly be lowered, without waiting for mobile steps to arrive.

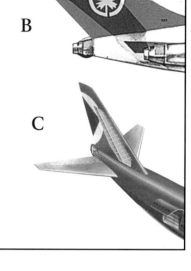

A

B

C

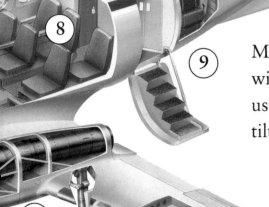

11. AILERONS

Movable sections on the wing's trailing edge are used to control lift and to tilt the plane for turning.

13. RUDDER

The rudder, together with the ailerons, controls the plane's direction.

14. RIBS

A series of vertical ribs gives the fin its strength.

15. WINDOWS

The windows on planes are usually small and round, to retain the strength of the fuselage.

10. TAIL

The tail is mounted high to keep it out of the air that is disturbed when it flows over the wings.

12. ELEVATORS

The angle of the plane as it flies is controlled mainly by the elevators on the tail plane.

16. GALLEY

Where meals are made.

INDEX

The finished
model glider

Answers: Pages 28–29
1 Apart from drag, they would fall at the same rate. **2** To make the air flow faster over the top, reducing its pressure, and providing lift. **3** A rocket produces the most thrust, but only for a few minutes, because it has to carry all its fuel with it. **4** The triangular shape is strongest as forces acting on it have to squash the card, as well as bend it. **Page 30** Tornado = B, 747 = E, Martin X-24B = A **Page 31** A = X–15, B = Tristar, C = 747.

PHOTO CREDITS
Abbreviations – t – top, m– middle, b – bottom, r – right, l – left, c – center:
Page 4 – Lufthansa, Bildarchiv; 5 – Pan Am; 7 & 23 – British Aerospace; 13 both & 27m – Airbus Industrie; 18 Rolls Royce plc; 26 Frank Spooner Pictures; 27mr – Civil Aviation Authority.

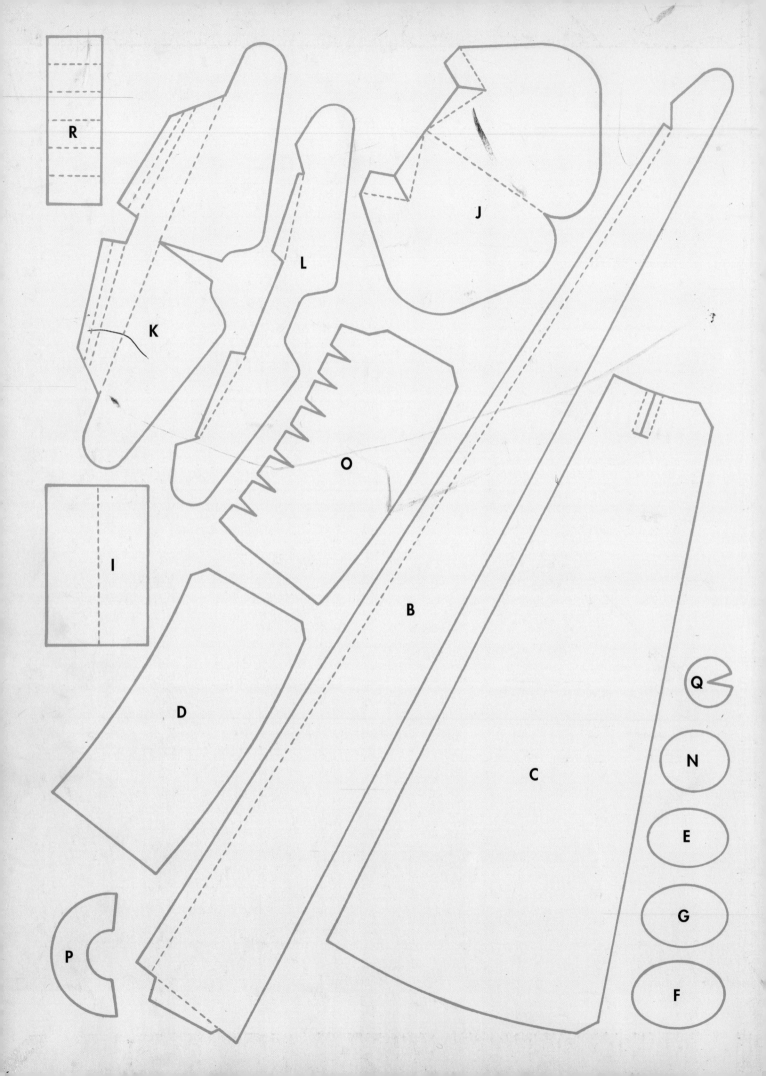